THE CALM BOOK

ALEX
ALLAN

ANNE
WILSON

WELBECK

Published in 2021 by Welbeck Children's Books
An imprint of Welbeck Children's Limited,
part of Welbeck Publishing Group
20 Mortimer Street, London W1T 3JW

Designer: Kathryn Davies
Art Editor: Deborah Vickers
Editor: Jenni Lazell
Consultant: Sarah Davis
Production: Gary Hayes

ISBN: 978-1-78312-651-4

Printed in Dongguan, China
9 8 7 6 5 4 3 2 1

Consultant Sarah Davis is a (UKCP registered)
psychotherapist with an MA in Integrative Child and
Adolescent Psychotherapy and Counselling.

She currently works in the voluntary sector
counseling and supporting young people to improve
their mental wellbeing. She has also worked as
a children's editor and consultant.

HOW ARE YOU **FEELING** TODAY?

HOW ARE YOU FEELING TODAY?

Are you **ENERGETIC**...

...and *bouncy*?

Are you **BRIGHT**

and **BUZZY**?

Or do you feel *tired* and *lazy*, or **MAD** and **GRUMPY**?

Maybe you feel

wobbly

and

shaky

and want to pull the blankets over your head?

Think about how you are feeling **INSIDE** and **OUT**.
Understanding what is going on inside your brain
and your body can help you stay C A L M so you
can deal with **WHATEVER** the day brings.

UNDERSTANDING YOUR BRAIN

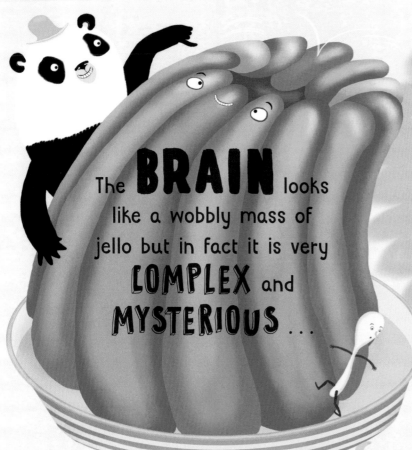

The **BRAIN** looks like a wobbly mass of jello but in fact it is very **COMPLEX** and **MYSTERIOUS** ...

Learning about how your brain works can help you understand your feelings better.

THE PREFRONTAL CORTEX

("pre-front-al kor-teks")
This is the part right at the front of your head, just behind your eyes. This part of the brain helps you think clearly and stay organized.

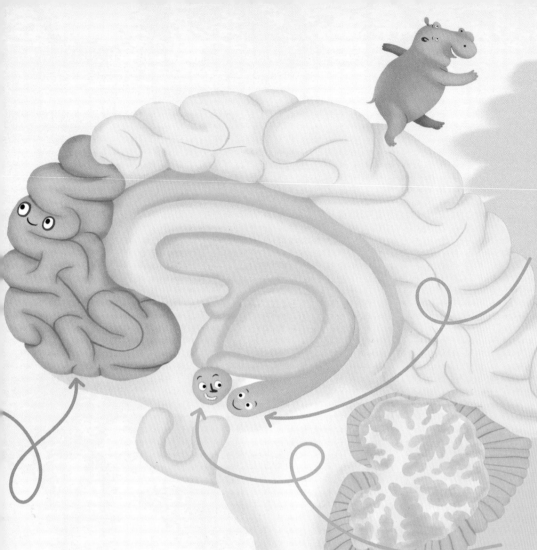

THE HIPPOCAMPUS

("hip-oh-cam-pus")
This part of the brain is shaped like a seahorse tail. It organizes and stores memories so you can use them when you need them.

THE AMYGDALA

("ah-mig-da-la")
This is a teeny, tiny part of the brain, right near the hippocampus. It might be small but it can TAKE OVER when it thinks you are in danger! This is called the "fight or flight" response, which we all need for survival.

When you are **CALM** you can . . .

- Think clearly
- Have a sensible chat
- Make good decisions
- Organize things and get to places on time

When you are calm, your **PREFRONTAL CORTEX** is in charge,
so it's easy to listen and learn, and to store up knowledge, positive
emotions, and memory in your **HIPPOCAMPUS**.

If things start to go **wrong**, our
prefrontal cortex is there to tell
us not to worry, to stay calm.

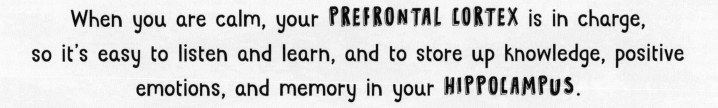

But sometimes our **fears** and **worries**
feel so terrifying that we can't seem
to keep calm. Before we know it,
the mighty **AMYGDALA** has taken over!

If we are ever in real danger, it's our **AMYGDALA** that gets us ready to

FIGHT

if we have to . . .

. . . or *RUN AWAY* as *fast* as we can.

(VERY USEFUL if a gigantic BEAR is chasing you!)

10

Our heart pumps faster, so the blood can flow to our muscles, making us **SUPER STRONG!** We breathe faster to get more oxygen, and the pupils of our eyes get bigger so we can see better.

Signs your amygdala might be in charge:

- Racing heartbeat making you feel jumpy
- Shortness of breath, making it hard to speak
- Pent-up energy making you want to run, kick, or shout
- Hot or sweaty hands
- Goosebumps on your skin

(NOT VERY USEFUL if the bear turns out to be NOT so scary!)

Once the **AMYGDALA** is in charge it can be very hard to calm it down. And then we might do things we wouldn't normally do, things that might seem silly, which makes us feel even worse . . .

. . . and we **CAN'T LISTEN TO ANYONE** who tries to help us!

AARRGGHHH!!!!!!!!!!

If we take **LONG, SLOW, DEEP BREATHS** the amygdala starts to listen to our prefrontal cortex saying...

...it's okay, we've got this, calm down.

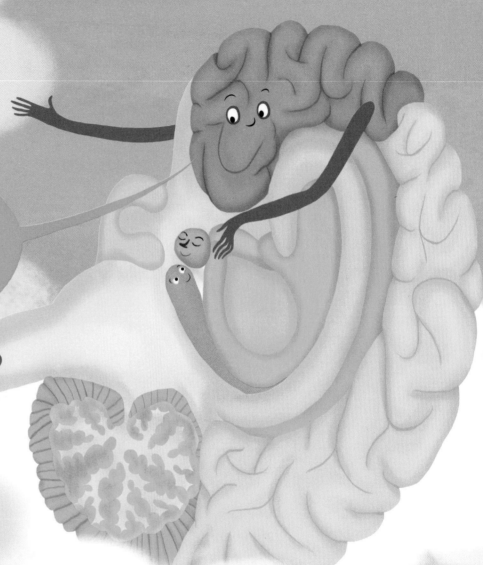

Try breathing in through your nose while counting 1, 2, 3, 4. Hold your breath for 1, 2, 3, 4, then breathe out through your mouth for 1, 2, 3, 4.

Soon, there's enough oxygen for the rest of the brain to start to work again.

DEEP BREATHING

is a great way to get you ready
for a good night's sleep.

All this brain activity can be exhausting,
so sometimes you might feel tired and
worn out. It helps to rest and recharge
your brain for the next day.

1. Lie down comfortably
on your back, ready to
do some DEEP BREATHING.
Imagine your tummy
is like a balloon.

2. Breathe in deeply to inflate the balloon as big as it can go, then slowly and gently blow out until the balloon is completely deflated again.

3. Try balancing a stuffed toy on top of your tummy—as you fill up the balloon it will gently lift up, and then as you exhale it will slowly drop down.

Repeat this as many times as you like until you—and your toy—start to feel more relaxed and sleepy.

15

We get better at anything the more we practice, so it can help to train your breathing for the next time you need to calm down. Here are some fun breathing exercises you can do every day.

BREATHE WITH A FRIEND

Sit back-to-back with a friend. Breathe in deeply, and exhale slowly ... listen for the breath and feel the rise and fall. Take turns to match your breathing to your friend.

BLOW ON A FEATHER

Breathe in and hold it for a count of 1, 2, 3 . . . and then breathe out, blowing up on one side of the feather and down the other side. Watch the edges of the feather move and settle with your breath.

BLOW BUBBLES

Concentrate on breathing in. Then steadily and gently breathe out through the bubble wand to make tiny bubbles appear. You can even close your eyes and blow bubbles in your imagination.

MINDFULNESS

can be a good way to train
your brain to be calm.

MINDFULNESS just means noticing
what is going on around you by
slowing down and paying attention
to things. Like this . . .

1. Sit down comfortably.

2. Take a deep breath and tighten all your muscles. Make every part of your body stiff and strong.

3. Clench your shoulders, ball your fists, crinkle up your toes. Hold this for as long as you can.

4. Now slowly breathe out as you start to let your toes loosen, your hands go floppy and your shoulders drop.

It might feel funny at first, but notice how much calmer you feel once you've let your body go all wiggly.

You can be **MINDFUL** by paying attention to all **FIVE SENSES**.

What can you **SEE?**

Find **five** things that you can see around you and describe them. Book, chair, window, cup, table . . .

What can you **FEEL?**

Find four things you can feel and describe them. Warm socks, soft pillow, scratchy rug, cool breeze . . .

What can you **HEAR?**

Listen out for **three** things. Can you hear traffic noise, birds singing, your own breathing . . .

What can you **SMELL?**

Can you notice *two* different smells? If not, think of two smells that you really like!

What can you **TASTE?**

Can you taste anything? If not, name your **favorite** taste!

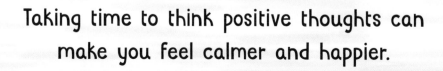

Taking time to think positive thoughts can make you feel calmer and happier.

GET MOVING and try some simple **YOGA** to improve memory and focus, and make you feel calm and relaxed.

Remember to take deep, relaxing breaths.

Imagine you are sitting cross-legged on a **CLOUD.** Breathe in and sit tall, with the palms of your hands on your knees.

Slowly reach your arms out in front of you, like a **TURTLE** coming out of his shell. Hello!

Curl up like a MOUSE.

First sit up on your heels and then slowly bring your head down in front of your knees, resting your arms by your sides.

Then move up onto your hands and knees, lift your head and arch your back like a FOX.

Or you can slowly round your back and tuck your head into your chest like a CAT.

Leave your hands in front of you and try lifting your bottom into the air and straightening your legs like a DOG.

YOGA is a great way to practice your **BREATHING**.
Try breathing in and out slowly for five breaths
in each of these yoga positions.

Stand up tall with your legs slightly apart, feet facing forward, and hands by your sides.

When you're ready, reach your arms as high as you can like a **GIRAFFE**.

Or drop from the waist and swing your arms low like an **ELEPHANT'S TRUNK**.

You can even try bringing one of your feet up to rest on the inside of your other leg like a **FLAMINGO**. Try not to wobble!

Now lie on your tummy like a **SNAKE** and stretch out your arms by your sides.

SSSSSsssssssssssss

Try putting your palms down near your shoulders and pulling yourself up like a **SEA LION**.

Arp arp arp!

Finally, lie flat on your back with your arms by your sides and breathe freely ...

Aaahh c a l m .

Taking time to **CREATE SOMETHING SPECIAL** can be a good way to calm down.

Try making a **GLITTER JAR** which you can use to cheer yourself up when you are feeling upset or when you just want to take some time out to unwind.

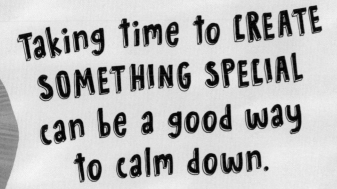

Shake the finished jar as hard as you can and then relax as you watch the tiny sparkles gently settle, until all is calm again.

All you need to make your own calm down glitter jar:

- A plastic jar with a lid that can be screwed on tight

- About half a cup of glitter glue or clear glue

- Distilled water (so it won't go mouldy!)

- A few teaspoons of extra glitter or sparkles

Add all the ingredients to the jar, close tight, and shake well.

TIP

You may want to seal the jar with tape if you're going to shake it REALLY HARD!

If you're feeling **WORRIED** or **UPSET** about something, it can help to squeeze a stress ball or squash some slime while you try to calm down.

Why not create your own **CALM** by making a squishy stress ball from a balloon ...

You will need:

- A balloon

- Some rice or flour

- A funnel

Fill the balloon with rice or flour using the funnel and tie tightly. You can ask a grown-up to help you tie the balloon. Then you can decorate it and get squishing!

Try making this easy **SLIME** out of simple kitchen ingredients.

You will need:

- 1/2 cup cornstarch

- 6–6 1/2 tablespoons of water

- food coloring

Add a few drops of food coloring to a little of the water, and add to the cornstarch gradually, mixing all the while. As you add more water it will become gooey! You can squash your slime into a ball, or watch it drip through your fingers.

Now you know what calm feels like, can you think of something **YOU** enjoy that makes you feel **CALM?**

Maybe . . .

Walking the dog or spending time with animals.

Being in a special, safe place, like a den.